NAME YOUR FAVORITE . . .

700 Rapid-Fire Ice Breakers to Get Teenagers Talking

Provoke even more conversation in your youth group with these quick-question discussion starters from Youth Specialties!

Would You Rather...?
465 Provocative Questions to Get Teenagers Talking
Doug Fields

Have You Ever...?
450 Intriguing Questions Guaranteed to Get Teenagers Talking
Les Christie

What If...?
450 Thought-Provoking Questions to Get Teenagers Talking, Laughing, and Thinking
Les Christie

Unfinished Sentences
450 Tantalizing Statement-Starters to Get Teenagers Talking & Thinking
Les Christie

NAME
YOUR
FAVORITE . . .

700 Rapid-Fire Ice Breakers to Get Teenagers Talking

Shawn Edwards
Don Stricklin
Gay Stricklin

Youth Specialties

WWW.ZONDERVAN.COM

NAME YOUR FAVORITE . . .
700 Rapid-Fire Ice Breakers to Get
Teenagers Talking

Copyright © 2002 by Youth Specialties

Youth Specialties Books, 300 S. Pierce St., El Cajon CA
92020, are published by Zondervan Publishing House,
5300 Patterson Ave. S.E., Grand Rapids MI 49530.

ISBN 0-310-24197-9
Edited by Rick Marschall
Cover and Interior design by Proxy, www.proxydesign.com

Printed in the United States of America
03 04 05 06 07 / / 10 9 8 7 6 5 4 3

TABLE OF CONTENTS

INTRODUCTION

I have been asked to write a Guest Introduction to this wonderful little book. I would count it as one of the honors of my career—I could even Name it as my Favorite compliment—except for two facts (to let you in on a couple of secrets): I am the Editor of the book; and I am the one who asked me to write this.

Nevertheless, it is a wonderful little book, as you will discover soon, starting a couple of pages to the right. I can tell you why, from personal experience. When I host Focus Groups at our great Youth Specialties conventions, I ask youth workers what their favorite YS resources are—what works the best? In truth I expect raves about our multi-media extravaganzas but—although the bells-and-whistle projects do help ministries in multitudinous ways—the frequent first answer is: Those Quick Question books!

Before we can go about the work of touching kids' lives for Jesus, to ground them in the Word, to do all the equipping, inspiring, encouraging that are the "main" parts of our job descriptions... we've got to get them comfortable. Isn't it funny? After a certain point, some kids will talk about their friendship with Jesus day and night. But once upon a time these same kids wouldn't talk to you or to each other; it was tough work to get them to open up or laugh. There are some nights that your youth group resembles a hillside of Easter Island statues. You know what I'm talking about!

Well, relief is on the way! We have designed this book so you can make notes and keep lists next to the 700 topics. Read them in order or jump around. Use these ice-breakers rapid-fire, or linger on kids' varied answers and watch discussion flow. You'll see: these will excite laughter, and they will prompt tears. Youth will go from sharing to caring. Listen closely: you'll hear some spiritual bells and whistles in those modest little pages.

Rick Marschall

1	...ACRONYM (NAME THIS ONE ASAP!)
2	...ACTOR
3	...ACTION MOVIE
4	...ACTRESS
5	...AESOP'S FABLE

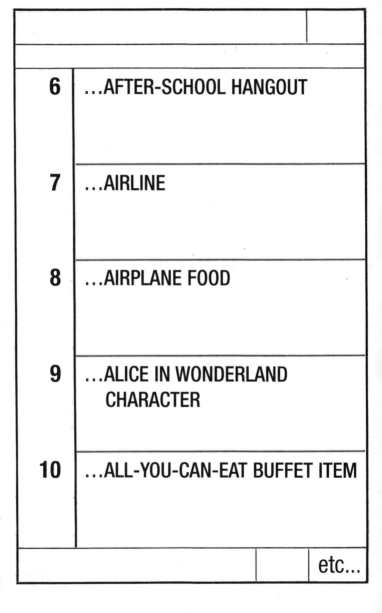

6	...AFTER-SCHOOL HANGOUT
7	...AIRLINE
8	...AIRPLANE FOOD
9	...ALICE IN WONDERLAND CHARACTER
10	...ALL-YOU-CAN-EAT BUFFET ITEM

etc...

11	…AMUSEMENT PARK RIDE
12	…ANECDOTE ABOUT SOMEONE'S INCREDIBLE ACT OF CHRISTIAN LOVE
13	…ANIMAL NAMED IN THE BIBLE
14	…ANIMAL SOUND OR CALL
15	…ANIMAL YOU'D LIKE TO BE FOR A DAY

21	…ARTIST
22	…ARTS AND CRAFTS PROJECT AT CAMP OR VBS
23	…APRIL FOOL'S DAY PRANK PULLED ON YOU
24	…APRIL FOOL'S DAY PRANK YOU'VE PULLED ON SOMEONE ELSE
25	…ASTRONAUT

26	...ATHLETE OR SPORTS STAR
27	...ATHLETE WHO HAS BEEN ARRESTED
28	...AUTHOR
29	...AWARDS SHOW
30	...BABY AT CHURCH

31	...BABY-FOOD FLAVOR
32	...BABYSITTER
33	...BAD ADVICE YOU'VE EVER RECEIVED OR GIVEN
34	...BAD MOVIE
35	...BAD SMELL

61	...BLUES SONG
62	...BBQ'd MEAT
63	...BOARD GAME
64	...BODY PART
65	...BODY PART TO PIERCE

66	...BONE TO CRACK
67	...BOOK OF THE BIBLE
68	...BOOK YOU LIKE TO RE-READ
69	...BOOK YOU WERE FORCED TO READ FOR SCHOOL
70	...BORING TEACHER

71	...BOTTLED WATER BRAND
72	...BOY BAND
73	...BRADY BUNCH EPISODE
74	...BRANCH OF MILITARY
75	...BRAND OF CATSUP

76	...BRAND OF FRENCH FRIES
77	...BRAND OF SUNGLASSES
78	...BRAND OF TOOTHPASTE
79	...BREAKFAST FOOD
80	...BREED OF DOG

81	...BUG
82	...BUMPER STICKER PHRASE
83	...CABLE CHANNEL
84	...CAMERA
85	...CAMP

91	...CAR GAME
92	...CARBONATED DRINK (AND YOUR FAVORITE NAME: SODA, POP, SOFT DRINK?)
93	...CARD GAME
94	...CARTOON DOG
95	...CARTOON THEME MUSIC

96	...CASSEROLE
97	...CAT NAME
98	...CATALOG TO ORDER FROM
99	...CD
100	...CEREAL MASCOT

101	…CHARACTER TO BE IN CLUE!
102	…CHARITY
103	…CHILD ACTOR
104	…CHILDHOOD FAMILY CAR
105	…CHILDHOOD TOY

131	…COMEBACK ROCK GROUP
132	…COMEDIAN
133	…COME-FROM-BEHIND WIN
134	…COMFORT FOOD
135	…COMMANDMENT

141	…COMPUTER FONT
142	…CONCERT YOU'VE EVER BEEN TO
143	…CONDIMENT
144	…CONSTELLATION
145	…CONVENIENCE STORE

146	…CORPORATE LOGO
147	…COSMETIC BRAND
148	…COUNTRY FLAG
149	…COUNTRY SINGER
150	…COUNTRY YOU'D LIKE TO LIVE IN

151	...COUNTRY YOU'D LIKE TO VISIT
152	...COUSIN
153	...CREEPY VOICE
154	...CUPCAKE FLAVOR
155	...CUTE OLD COUPLE AT CHURCH

156	...DANCE MOVE (PLEASE DEMONSTRATE)
157	...DANCE YOU'D LIKE TO LEARN
158	...DAY OF THE WEEK
159	...DEAD ACTOR
160	...DEAD MUSICIAN

181	…DISNEY VILLAIN
182	…DOCTOR OR NURSE
183	…DOLLAR-STORE ITEM
184	…DONUT
185	…DOWNTOWN BUILDING OR SKYSCRAPER

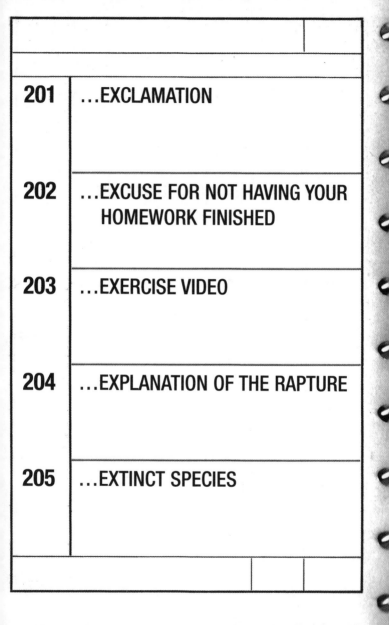

211	...FAMILY TRADITION
212	...FAMILY VACATION
213	...FAMILY-REUNION GAME
214	...FAMOUS PERSON YOU WISH YOU WERE RELATED TO
215	...FAST-FOOD RESTAURANT

221	…FISH
222	…FLAVOR OF COUGH SYRUP
223	…FLOWER
224	…FLU REMEDY
225	…FOLK HERO

231	…FOOD TO MIX TOGETHER
232	…FOOD YOUR GRANDMOTHER MAKES
233	…FOREIGN COUNTRY
234	…FOREIGN CURRENCY
235	…FOREIGN MOVIE

236	…FOREIGN WORD OR PHRASE
237	…FORM OF POTATO (FRIES, HASH BROWNS, TATER TOTS, ETC.)
238	…FOUNDING FATHER (OF THE US)
239	…FREE-TIME ACTIVITY
240	…FRIEND

241	...FROZEN DRINK
242	...FROZEN TREAT
243	...FRUIT
244	...FUNNY NAME OF A TOWN OR CITY
245	...FUNNY VOICE OF A CLERK, TEACHER, OR STRANGER

251	...GAME YOU PLAYED AT SCHOOL WHEN THE WEATHER WAS TOO BAD TO GO OUTSIDE
252	...GAS STATION
253	...GATORADE FLAVOR
254	...GEM
255	...GET-UP-AND-DANCE PRAISE SONG

256	…GIFT FROM GOD
257	…GIFT TO GIVE
258	…GIRL SCOUT COOKIE
259	…GOOD ADVICE YOU'VE EVER RECEIVED OR GIVEN
260	…GOSPEL SONG THAT ALMOST ALWAYS BRINGS TEARS TO YOUR EYES

261	…GRANDPARENT'S OR ANCIENT RELATIVE'S NAME
262	…GREAT BUY FOR UNDER $10
263	…GREEN THING ON ST PATRICK'S DAY
264	…GYM UNIFORM
265	…HAIKU

266	...HAIR COLOR
267	...HAIR PRODUCT
268	...HAIRSTYLE FROM THE PAST
269	...HAIRPIECE (WITHOUT NAMING THE PERSON WHO WEARS IT!)
270	...HALLOWEEN COSTUME

301	...INSPIRATIONAL BOOK
302	...INSPIRATIONAL SPEAKER
303	...INSTRUMENT YOU'D LIKE TO LEARN TO PLAY
304	...INTERNATIONAL CONFLICT
305	...INVENTION FROM THE 20TH CENTURY

306	...INVENTION THAT YOU'RE DYING TO BRING TO THE WORLD
307	...INVENTOR
308	...ITEM IN YOUR BEDROOM
309	...ITEM IN YOUR PURSE OR WALLET
310	...ITEM MADE OF PLASTIC

311	...ITEM ON A SALAD BAR THAT YOU NEVER SEE AT HOME
312	...ITEM TO PUT INTO A TIME CAPSULE THAT WOULD REPRESENT YOU
313	...JAZZ MUSICIAN
314	...JELLYBEAN FLAVOR
315	...JOKE

316	...JUNK FOOD
317	...JUNK MAIL
318	...KID TO BABY SIT
319	...KIND OF CHEESE
320	...KIND OF PANCAKE

321	…KIND OF WEATHER
322	…KNOCK-KNOCK JOKE
323	…KNOT
324	…KODAK MOMENT
325	…KOOL-AID FLAVOR

361	...MOMENT IN HISTORY
362	...MOMENT DURING A NEW YEAR'S CELEBRATION
363	...MONTH OF THE YEAR
364	...MORNING RITUAL
365	...MOST CONFUSING ITEM ON A COFFEE-BAR MENU

371	...MOVIE MUSICAL
372	...MOVIE PREVIEW
373	...MOVIE SOUNDTRACK
374	...MOVIE YOU'VE SEEN IN THE PAST MONTH
375	...MR. ROGERS'S SWEATER

381	…MYTHOLOGICAL FIGURE
382	…NAME FOR A BOY
383	…NAME FOR A GIRL
384	…NAME FOR JESUS
385	…NAME FOR A DOG

386	...NAME FOR A DOLL
387	...NAME FOR A BIRD
388	...NAME OF A VEGETABLE
389	...NASCAR DRIVER
390	...NATIONAL PARK

396	...NEWSPAPER
397	...NIGHT OF TV
398	...NIGHTMARE (OR LEAST FAVORITE!)
399	...NOISE TO MAKE WITH YOUR BODY
400	...NONSENSE WORD

401	…NUMBER
402	…NUMBER OF SIBLINGS TO HAVE
403	…NURSERY RHYME
404	…OLD TESTAMENT PROPHET
405	…OLYMPIC SPORT

411	...OVERUSED PHRASE OR WORD OF YOUR YOUTH MINISTER
412	...PAINTING
413	...PAIR OF PAJAMAS
414	...PAIR OF SHOES
415	...PAIR OF UNDERWEAR

421	…PASTOR, PRIEST, OR CLERGY MEMBER
422	…PEANUTS CHARACTER
423	…PERFUME/COLOGNE
424	…PERSON TO TAKE A ROAD TRIP WITH
425	…PERSON TO TAKE CARE OF YOU WHEN YOU ARE SICK

426	...PERSON WHO INSPIRES YOU
427	...PERSON YOU WANT TO SEE IN HEAVEN
428	...PERSON YOU'D MOST LIKE TO PLAY "YOU" IN A MOVIE ABOUT YOU
429	...PET PEEVE
430	...PET YOU'VE EVER HAD

436	...PILLOW
437	...PIZZA TOPPING
438	...PLACE TO BE ALONE WITH GOD
439	...PLACE TO BE STUCK IN TRAFFIC
440	...PLACE TO BUY BOOKS

441	...PLACE TO BUY CDS
442	...PLACE TO BUY CLOTHES
443	...PLACE TO BUY SHOES
444	...PLACE TO GO FISHING
445	...PLACE YOU'VE HIDDEN EASTER EGGS

456	...POLITICIAN
457	...POPSICLE COLOR OR FLAVOR
458	...POSTER
459	...POTATO-CHIP FLAVOR
460	...PRACTICAL JOKE

461	...PRAISE AND WORSHIP SONG
462	...PRAYER (MEMORIZED OR FROM PRAYER-BOOK OR HYMNAL)
463	...PRAYER-PARTNER
464	...PRESIDENT OR VICE PRESIDENT
465	...PRESIDENTIAL JOKE

481	...RELIGION OR DENOMINATION YOU'D LIKE TO LEARN MORE ABOUT
482	...REPTILE
483	...RESTAURANT (HOLE IN THE WALL)
484	...RETRO HAIRSTYLE
485	...RIDICULOUS TABLOID-NEWSPAPER HEADLINE

486	...RICH PERSON IN THE NEWS
487	...RIDDLE
488	...ROAD KILL
489	...ROAD SIGN
490	...ROAD TRIP FOOD OR SNACK

491	…RODENT
492	…RODEO EVENT
493	…ROMANTIC MOVIE
494	…"ROSES ARE RED, VIOLETS ARE BLUE…" RHYME
495	…ROOM OF YOUR HOUSE

496	...SAINT
497	...SALAD DRESSING
498	...SANDWICH
499	...SATURDAY MORNING CARTOON
500	...SCAR (TELL STORY BEHIND IT)

501	...SCARIEST ANIMAL STORY
502	...SCARY STORY TO TELL
503	...SCHOOL CAFETERIA FOOD
504	...SCHOOL CHEER
505	...SCHOOL FIELD TRIP

511	...SEAFOOD
512	...SEARCH ENGINE
513	...SEASON TO DRESS FOR
514	...SEAT ON THE BUS
515	...SECTION OF STANDARDIZED TESTS

516	…SECTION OF THE NEWSPAPER
517	…SEINFELD EPISODE
518	…SEQUEL
519	…SERMON
520	…SERMON TOPIC THAT YOU WOULD PREACH ON

521	...SESAME STREET CHARACTER
522	...SHAMPOO
523	...SHAPE OF A SWIMMING POOL
524	...SHAPE OF BAND-AID
525	...SHIRTSLEEVE LENGTH

526	...SHOPPING MALL
527	...SICKNESS
528	...SIMPSONS CHARACTER
529	...SITCOM YOU'D LIKE TO BE A CHARACTER ON
530	...SKI TRIP

531	…SKI TRIP CRASH STORY
532	…SLANG WORD OR PHRASE
533	…SLEEPOVER OR SLUMBER PARTY
534	…SLOGAN WRITTEN ON A CHURCH SIGN
535	…SLOW-DANCE SONG

536	...SMELL
537	...SMURF
538	...SNOW-CONE FLAVOR
539	...SOAP
540	...SOAP OPERA

541	..."SOMEONE'S SNEAKING A SMOKE" STORY
542	...SON OF JACOB
543	...SONG DEDICATED TO YOUR SCHOOL OR STATE
544	...SONG FROM THE '80S
545	...SONG FROM THE '90S

546	...SONG TO DANCE TO
547	...SONG TO GET YOU OUT OF A BAD MOOD
548	...SONG TO SING IN THE SHOWER
549	...SOUP
550	...SPAGHETTI SAUCE

551	...SPAM RECIPE
552	...SPANISH PRONOUN
553	...SPECIAL-EFFECTS MOVIE
554	...SPECTATOR SPORT
555	...SPEED LIMIT

556	...SPICE
557	...SPICY FOOD
558	...SPORT
559	...SPORTS LOGO
560	...SPORTS MASCOT

561	...SPORTS MOMENT THAT YOU SAW LIVE
562	...SPORTS MOVIE
563	...STAINED-GLASS WINDOW IN A CHURCH
564	...STATE CAPITOL
565	...STATE YOU'D LIKE TO LIVE IN

571	...STORY OF ONE PERSON'S SACRIFICE FOR ANOTHER
572	...STORY TO HAVE READ TO YOU
573	...STORY YOUR GRANDPARENTS TELL ABOUT YOU OVER AND OVER
574	...STRANGE FLOAT OR THEME IN A PARADE
575	...STREET NAME

576	…STUNT
577	…STYLE OF HAT
578	…SUBJECT IN SCHOOL
579	…SUBSTITUTE TEACHER
580	…SUGAR-COATED CEREAL

581	...STUFFED ANIMAL
582	...SUMMER CAMP COUNSELOR
583	...SUMMER CAMP GAME
584	...SUMMER CAMP MEAL
585	...SUMMER CAMP MEMORY

586	...SUMMER CAMP SILLY SONG
587	...SUMMER OF YOUR LIFE
588	...SUMMER SPORT
589	...SUMO WRESTLER (OR MATCH YOU'VE WATCHED)
590	...SUNBURN STORY

591	...SUNDAY FUNNIES CHARACTER
592	...SUNDAY-SCHOOL LESSON
593	...SUNDAY-SCHOOL TEACHER
594	...SUPER BOWL COMMERCIAL
595	...SUPER HERO

601	...TALENT YOU DON'T HAVE, BUT WOULD LIKE TO HAVE
602	...TALENT YOU HAVE
603	...TALK SHOW
604	...TALL TALE
605	...TEACHER

606	...TELEVANGELIST HAIRSTYLE
607	...TELEVISION JUDGE
608	...TENNIS PLAYER
609	...THING ABOUT THE AGE YOU ARE
610	...THING ABOUT YOURSELF THAT WOULD SURPRISE OTHERS

611	…THING ABOUT YOUR DAD
612	…THING ABOUT YOUR MOM
613	…THING TO DO ON A COLD DAY
614	…THING TO DO ON A HOT DAY
615	…THING THAT'S HAPPENED TO YOU TODAY

616	...THING TO DO ON A RAINY DAY
617	...THING TO DO ON AN AIRPLANE
618	...THING TO DO WITH A RUBBER BAND
619	...THING TO EAT WITH PEANUT BUTTER
620	...THING TO DO WITH YOUR DAD OR MOM

621	...THING TO HANG FROM YOUR REAR-VIEW MIRROR
622	...THING YOU LOOK FORWARD TO ABOUT BEING A PARENT
623	...THING YOU LOOK FORWARD TO ABOUT BEING IN COLLEGE
624	...THING YOU LOVE ABOUT BEING FROM YOUR CITY/STATE
625	...THING YOU WANT TO DO BEFORE YOU GRADUATE

626	...TICKLISH SPOT
627	...TIME TO PRAY
628	...TIME YOU DIED LAUGHING
629	...TIME YOU GOT GROUNDED
630	...TIME YOU THREW UP

631	…TIME YOU WANTED TO, LIKE, DISOWN YOUR PARENTS OUT OF EMBARRASSMENT
632	…TIME YOU WERE REALLY, REALLY IN THE WRONG!
633	…TOE
634	…TOENAIL POLISH COLOR
635	…TOILET-PAPER BRAND

636	...TOILETRY OR BATHROOM ITEM
637	...TONGUE TWISTER
638	...TOOTHPASTE BRAND
639	...TREE
640	...TRIP TO THE HOSPITAL

641	...TRUCK STOP
642	...T-SHIRT
643	...TV DAD
644	...TV PERSONALITY YOU HAD A CRUSH ON WHEN YOU WERE LITTLE
645	...TV SHOW FROM THE '70S

646	...TV SHOW YOU WATCH BUT WOULD NEVER ADMIT IT
647	...TV SIDEKICK
648	...TV THEME SONG
649	...TYPE OF CAR
650	...TYPE OF CHEESE

651	...TYPE OF CRACKER
652	...TYPE OF EXERCISE
653	...TYPE OF FIREWORK
654	...TYPE OF LETTUCE
655	...TYPE OF POETRY TO WRITE

656	...UNAPPRECIATED OR UNDISCOVERED BAND
657	...UNCOMFORTABLE CLOTHING
658	...UNDERDEVELOPED COUNTRY
659	...UNSOLVED MYSTERY
660	...UNSUNG HERO

661	..."URBAN LEGEND"
662	...USELESS SCHOOL ASSEMBLY
663	...VACATION LOCATION
664	...VALENTINE
665	...VALUE OR TRAIT TO HAVE

671	…WATER SPORT
672	…WAY TO EAT AN EGG
673	…WAY TO EAT SHRIMP
674	…WAY TO NOT STUDY
675	…WAY TO SAY "HELLO"

681	...WINNIE THE POOH CHARACTER
682	...WINTER SPORT
683	...WIZARD OF OZ CHARACTER
684	...WOMAN OF THE BIBLE
685	...WONDER OF THE WORLD

NOTES . . .

RESOURCES FROM YOUTH SPECIALTIES

Ideas Library
Ideas Library on CD-ROM 2.0
Administration, Publicity, & Fundraising
Camps, Retreats, Missions, & Service Ideas
Creative Meetings, Bible Lessons, & Worship Ideas
Crowd Breakers & Mixers
Discussion & Lesson Starters
Discussion & Lesson Starters 2
Drama, Skits, & Sketches
Drama, Skits, & Sketches 2
Drama, Skits, & Sketches 3
Games
Games 2
Games 3
Holiday Ideas
Special Events

Bible Curricula
Creative Bible Lessons from the Old Testament
Creative Bible Lessons in 1 & 2 Corinthians
Creative Bible Lessons in Galatians and Philippians
Creative Bible Lessons in John
Creative Bible Lessons in Romans
Creative Bible Lessons on the Life of Christ
Creative Bible Lessons in Psalms
Downloading the Bible Kit
Wild Truth Bible Lessons
Wild Truth Bible Lessons 2
Wild Truth Bible Lessons—Pictures of God

Topical Curricula
Creative Junior High Programs from A to Z, Vol. 1 (A-M)
Creative Junior High Programs from A to Z, Vol. 2 (N-Z)
Girls: 10 Gutsy, God-Centered Sessions on Issues that Matter to Girls
Guys: 10 Fearless, Faith-Focused Sessions on Issues that Matter to
Guys
Good Sex
Live the Life! Student Evangelism Training Kit
The Next Level Youth Leader's Kit
Roaring Lambs
So What Am I Gonna Do with My Life?
Student Leadership Training Manual
Student Underground
Talking the Walk
What Would Jesus Do? Youth Leader's Kit
Wild Truth Bible Lessons
Wild Truth Bible Lessons 2
Wild Truth Bible Lessons—Pictures of God

Discussion Starters
Discussion & Lesson Starters (Ideas Library)
Discussion & Lesson Starters 2 (Ideas Library)
EdgeTV
Every Picture Tells a Story
Get 'Em Talking
Keep 'Em Talking!
High School TalkSheets—Updated!
More High School TalkSheets—Updated!
High School TalkSheets from Psalms and Proverbs—Updated!
Junior High-Middle School TalkSheets—Updated!
More Junior High-Middle School TalkSheets—Updated!
Junior High-Middle School TalkSheets from Psalms and Proverbs—Updated!
Real Kids: Short Cuts
Real Kids: The Real Deal—on Friendship, Loneliness, Racism, & Suicide
Real Kids: The Real Deal—on Sexual Choices, Family Matters, & Loss
Real Kids: The Real Deal—on Stressing Out, Addictive Behavior, Great Comebacks, & Violence
Real Kids: Word on the Street
Small Group Qs
Have You Ever...?
Unfinished Sentences
What If...?
Would You Rather...?

Drama Resources
Drama, Skits, & Sketches (Ideas Library)
Drama, Skits, & Sketches 2 (Ideas Library)
Drama, Skits, & Sketches 3 (Ideas Library)
Dramatic Pauses
Spontaneous Melodramas
Spontaneous Melodramas 2
Super Sketches for Youth Ministry

Game Resources
Games (Ideas Library)
Games 2 (Ideas Library)
Games 3 (Ideas Library)
Junior High Game Nights
More Junior High Game Nights
Play It!
Screen Play CD-ROM

Additional Programming Resources
(also see Discussion Starters)
Camps, Retreats, Missions, & Service Ideas (Ideas Library)
Creative Meetings, Bible Lessons, & Worship Ideas (Ideas Library)
Crowd Breakers & Mixers (Ideas Library)
Everyday Object Lessons

Great Fundraising Ideas for Youth Groups
More Great Fundraising Ideas for Youth Groups
Great Retreats for Youth Groups
Great Talk Outlines for Youth Ministry
Holiday Ideas (Ideas Library)
Incredible Questionnaires for Youth Ministry
Kickstarters
Memory Makers
Special Events (Ideas Library)
Videos That Teach
Videos That Teach 2
Worship Services for Youth Groups

Digital Resources
Clip Art Library Version 2.0 (CD-ROM)
Great Talk Outlines for Youth Ministry
Hot Illustrations CD-ROM
Ideas Library on CD-ROM 2.0
Screen Play
Youth Ministry Management Tools

Videos & Video Curricula
Dynamic Communicators Workshop
EdgeTV
Live the Life! Student Evangelism Training Kit
Make 'Em Laugh!
Purpose-Driven® Youth Ministry Training Kit
Real Kids: Short Cuts
Real Kids: The Real Deal—on Friendship, Loneliness, Racism, & Suicide
Real Kids: The Real Deal—on Sexual Choices, Family Matters, & Loss
Real Kids: The Real Deal—on Stressing Out, Addictive Behavior, Great
Comebacks, & Violence
Real Kids: Word on the Street
Student Underground
Understanding Your Teenager Video Curriculum
Youth Ministry Outside the Lines

Especially for Junior High
Creative Junior High Programs from A to Z, Vol. 1 (A-M)
Creative Junior High Programs from A to Z, Vol. 2 (N-Z)
Junior High Game Nights
More Junior High Game Nights
Junior High-Middle School TalkSheets—Updated!
More Junior High-Middle School TalkSheets—Updated!
Junior High-Middle School TalkSheets from Psalms and Proverbs—
Updated!
Wild Truth Journal for Junior Highers
Wild Truth Bible Lessons
Wild Truth Bible Lessons 2
Wild Truth Journal—Pictures of God
Wild Truth Bible Lessons—Pictures of God

Student Resources
Downloading the Bible: A Rough Guide to the New Testament
Downloading the Bible: A Rough Guide to the Old Testament
Grow for It! Journal through the Scriptures
So What Am I Gonna Do with My Life?
Spiritual Challenge Journal: The Next Level
Teen Devotional Bible
What (Almost) Nobody Will Tell You about Sex
What Would Jesus Do? Spiritual Challenge Journal

Clip Art
Youth Group Activities (print)
Clip Art Library Version 2.0 (CD-ROM)

Quick Question Books
Have You Ever...?
Small Group Qs
Unfinished Sentences
What If...?
Would You Rather...?

Professional Resources
Administration, Publicity, & Fundraising (Ideas Library)
Dynamic Communicators Workshop
Great Talk Outlines for Youth Ministry
Help! I'm a Junior High Youth Worker!
Help! I'm a Small-Group Leader!
Help! I'm a Sunday School Teacher!
Help! I'm an Urban Youth Worker!
Help! I'm a Volunteer Youth Worker!
Hot Illustrations for Youth Talks
More Hot Illustrations for Youth Talks
Still More Hot Illustrations for Youth Talks
Hot Illustrations for Youth Talks 4
How to Expand Your Youth Ministry
How to Speak to Youth...and Keep Them Awake at the Same Time
Junior High Ministry (Updated & Expanded)
Make 'Em Laugh!
The Ministry of Nurture
Postmodern Youth Ministry
Purpose-Driven® Youth Ministry
Purpose-Driven® Youth Ministry Training Kit
So That's Why I Keep Doing This!
Teaching the Bible Creatively
A Youth Ministry Crash Course
Youth Ministry Management Tools
The Youth Worker's Handbook to Family Ministry

Academic Resources
Four Views of Youth Ministry & the Church
Starting Right
Youth Ministry That Transforms